X

Janette Voski

X Copyright © Janette Voski, 2021.
First published on 10 October 2020. (X X MMXX)
This version was published on 10 October 2021.

All rights reserved. No part of this book may be reproduced or transmitted in any form or by any means without written permission from the author.

ISBN: 978-0-6485925-9-4

Cover image of Janette Voski.
Cover image photography by Donna-Liza Piliu.
Cover image editing by Maria Lavorato and Janette Voski.

Also by Janette Voski

Bones

Thank you

Mama and Baba
For instilling strong values and morals. For providing a secure and happy home. For showing me that passion is an emotion more powerful when it is acted upon. For my brother and sister.

Minass
For the strength you encouraged in me from a very young age. You may underestimate the impact of your words, but I carry their weight everywhere I go.

Sometimes I ask myself, what would Minass do?

Mari
For leading by example in your loyalty, honesty, patience and unyielding spirit. You remind me every day I am *astonishing*… now I believe it.

Sometimes I ask myself, what would Mari do?

Contents

Preface 1

I: Expose 3

Drop It
Smokescreen
Social
Con Artist
Grace
Rumours
Lady
Narcissist
Fox
Unparalleled

II: Extricate 15

Done
Peripheral
Bad
Depth
Hey, Sailor
Lucid
Duplicity or Death
You
Pleonasm
Fire

III: Expire 27

Coaster
Iceberg
Die Baby, Die
Pea
Lone Wolf
Fanciful
Memory Lane
Brick Wall
Explosive
Last

Contents

IV: Express 39

Do You?
Strong
Two Way Street
Too
I'll Keep
Stuck
Another Language
XYZ
Three
Gogh

V: Excuse 51

Dark Night
Sick
Water
Forgive Yourself
Underdog
Stay With Me
Thunder
Navigate
Prickwork
XXXXX

VI: Execute 63

Little One
Don't
Spinning
Limit
Keep It
Original
Protagonist
Treasure
Puzzle
Climb

Contents

VII: Exhale 75

Free
Love
Bloom
Wild
Bones
Archery
Music
Inhale
Colours That Don't Exist
Numbers

VIII: Exude 87

She's The Woman
Peach Schnapps
Poker
Voski
Strawberry Conserve
Reflection
Artist
Blue Moon
Volcano
Magic

IX: Explore 99

Overpowering
Less Is More
Beauty
Spine
Dead Friends
Brain
Life
Equation
Rain
Snakes and Ladders

Contents

X: Exalt 111

Heaven
Dada
Nana
Morkouyr Janette
Earth
Baba
Mama
Minass
Mari
Home

X 123

Regret
Silence
The Sistine Chapel
She
Strangers
Cuddly
Sometimes
Cherry
Aveli
Pillow

Epilogue 135

X

Preface

The letter X is both powerful, and a paradox.

It is in our genetics, the X chromosomes we carry, yet trees are painted with an X when they are due to be cut down. The X is an unknown in algebra yet can be used to mark the spot of a hidden treasure. X symbolises a strike in bowling, a win, yet an X in softball can be used to mark a loss. XXX was written on jugs full of moonshine, yet X is used to identify a liquid poison. X can create a pattern in design, but X can also mean danger, do not enter. In animations an X over the eyes symbolises death, yet we use X to send kisses in text. The X in roman numerals symbolises the number ten, but the X in the alphabet is the twenty-fourth letter. X in faux is silent, but the letter X is the only consonant that has two parts to the sound that it makes – "e-ks".

To me, the letter X is simply a variable. The X symbolises what I have written, and more that I have not.

I never thought I would be on the receiving end of the situations I have. From broken friendships to bursts in relationships and everything else in between.

I have found myself staring directly into the face of a ticking timebomb and felt the pressure of having to defuse the explosive before detonation. Not always comprehending why the bomb was left in my hands, but always willing to explore it for insight.

I: Expose

What was to remain hidden, ultimately uncovered.

Even at a masquerade ball, you can still recognise the person behind the mask.

X

Drop It

Your selfless nature draws attention
You may feel your compassion traps you
Manipulation is a heavy bag of burden
But you are determined to make it through.

The truth – is this: you carry bags that weigh heavy
Some, their burden not yours
But the X on the labels read poison
And your limit is the cure.

Long term the toxic is chronic
It can eat away at your flesh
The only tonic to save yourself
Is to drop it and start afresh.

Your kind soul may seek to help
But learn that manipulation is not for you
Remember your strength frightens those
Who wish to see your rose cheeks turn blue.

The beauty – is this: to reach the next stage in life
You must rid the excess weight
Before it drags you backward
Before you freeze and stagnate.

One step back
Two steps forward
Drop the poison
Rose cheeks turn red.

X

Smokescreen

I wear it with a grin
Polka dots

I take a sip of sin
Amaretto shots

I raise your chin
Smile lots

I kiss your skin
Cherry knots

I see your guise wearing thin
Ink blots.

X

Social

The perfect groom and bride
A life where he never cried
Platform to inform or misguide
Rare profundity, she's dignified
Neglecting old friends, blatant snide
Lingerie showing her backside
Symbols and signs, superficial yet glorified
Innocent and naive all starry-eyed
Gain some weight, get crucified
Modify ourselves to feel verified
Smiles hiding sinister sides
Out to mingle, all preoccupied.

X

Con Artist

Conquest, your favourite, to
Conquer, you wish.
Conceal, tried often
Convince, and squish.

Confess, your wrongs, a
Contest, was this.
Consumed, in yourself
Conscience, you miss.

Conflict, you run, to
Confuse, your enjoyment.
Condemn, I did, and your
Control, never dormant.

Confectionary, turned sour
Congratulations, you're wicked.
Conversations, turned cold
Con artist, you're convicted.

X

Grace

If I took the memory of your pain away
Would you grace each day the same way?

X

Rumours

Today I learned not to believe everything I read.

I learned it because
They were talking about me.

X

Lady

I am about to speak
Words of misfortune

Instead, I hold my breath

Spit the words from my tongue
They land in my palm

I am no Lady Macbeth.

X

Narcissist

I write paragraphs to delete them
Hover over your name.
Remember the depth of my compassion
Where yours was just a game.

You made a name for yourself
By hurting those all around.
The more you spoke, I thought
Boy, how ridiculous you sound.

Suddenly, it clicked
I saw it all much clearer.
To you I measured less than what you saw
There in the mirror.

Reached my limit to count the times
I kicked the can down the road.
A prince? No, it was a facade
You were always a toad.

I left you in admiration
Walked away, head held high.
Now you can't reach me
Boy, don't even try.

X

Fox

Puppet master
Oh, the string was frayed
It snapped and I fell into the hay.

Slowly, like a snail
Your reality was crum-bling.

Your puppet: gone astray!

Quickly, like a fox, I jump
Your plan was un-rav-el-ling.

Your fix, to grip on me.

Do not test a fox, for she's a vixen.
Puppet master, now you're my prey.

X

Unparalleled

Wisdom is recognition of mistakes
Choosing not to repeat them.
Your appearance changed
As you became cold-hearted.

You remind me you're wise, you're handsome, you're a catch.

But reminders are for when we *actually* forget.

So I walk away to remind *you*…

You've met your match.

II: Extricate

Their grip tries to tighten.
How liberating it is to feel the weight lighten.

Done

You say you're done
You're not going to stay

You've been here before
Stuck on replay

If you could define him, he's like adrenaline
Fight on command

But when you draw the line
Is it within the sand?

So when the wind comes
And blows it away

It just delays your pain
A couple more days.

X

Peripheral

I was in your peripheral

                                        What I saw I vocalised

Coming from a different angle

                                        Careful not to criticise

I stepped back to state my logic
This time, more than just optics.

                                Corrections are not judgements
                                      They are improvements!

But your eyes rolled
My warning: redundant.

You never saw my perspective

More than through a mirror

                                        Be self-reflective!

Suddenly you seemed desensitised.

So you turned away, and

Shut your eyes.

X

Bad

You ever notice that all the bad things seem to happen to good people?

Perhaps there are no bad people.

Perhaps we categorise them incorrectly and expect too much.

Or perhaps we just don't hang around long enough to see that they never really get away with being beastly.

X

Depth

They might be shallow like a kiddy pool
And make waves with their hands

But you are as deep as the Pacific.

You rise and fall with the waves but
Know when to swim against the current.

You know your depth wasn't rewarded
Because your legs are still kicking.

And you remember what it was like
To reach your chin to the surface
Where the water would lap against your neck.

Did you know deep oceans bury shipwrecks?

X

Hey, Sailor

Although I am healed
I remain distant
Just like a shield
Protectively resistant.

Twelve years you were enlisted
My armour, heavy display
Warned soldiers' minds were twisted
But there was something, drawing me to stay.

We got to know each other more
Overcome by sonder, thoughts hurried
Your suffering from battle and war
Watching your friends get buried.

You were kind, and charming
You enjoyed my light and wit
What should have been alarming
Was your masterful skit.

Deceitful with your speech
Failing to connect words with meaning
As long as you allowed, I attempted to teach
Afflicted, your mind needed clearing.

You told me I was good, kind, and fun
A lady who was admirable for her inability to quit
Boy, you were like a loaded gun
Except you were full of shit.

X

Lucid

Sometimes I listen to white noise
Other times there's no sound and I'm trying to stay poised
Because music transcends time and place
I'm walking in slow motion, I'm rich, I'm famous

Wind swaying the curtains
As the sand gently shuffles
Yet I'm now standing still
And can't help but chuckle

Lift my shoulders and hear a crack
Take a step forward and never look back
Place strands of hair behind my ears
Smile remembering I'm facing my fears

I look to the horizon and my eyes adjust
Reach my arms wide, I just need to trust
My strength, my passion and fire from within
As hot as the wind against my skin

I take a dive
Finally feeling alive
I'm making my own sound, I'm making my own music
Its impact on my mind, it's making me lucid.

Duplicity or Death

Cobblestone pathway
Duplicity or death
Fork in the road
Almost no time left

Bite your lips
Then decide
Which way you'll go
Which way you'll ride

We are imperfectly perfect
Have our own troubles
Yet it's so easy to overlook them
When your own life feels like rubble

Blow out red
Breathe in blue
I choose the road with a cliff
I choose the road opposite you.

X

You

You thought she'd reach out
Because you always do.

You thought they'd honour your birthday
Because you make theirs a holiday.

You thought he'd stay your friend
Because you never left him to fend.

But darling, let me speak not to repeat
Sit back, slink into the backseat.

They don't hurt your feelings, your expectations do
Next time you make friends, don't change. Stay true.

X

Pleonasm

I finally realised that missing you is like using pleonasms.

Pointless.

X

Fire

Feed it with every breath
Like consuming fire.
Try to drown it with water
But it doesn't make a dent.

First understand, to forge steel
You must temper it with fire.
Channel your passion
No time for lament.

Pick up your sword
Symbol of battle
And strike a blow.

Hours pass
A sudden clash
You will not be overthrown.

Two swords land
Blades, into the ground
They decussate.
Celebrate the end.

But this was one of many
So do not turn blind.

Let the swords corrode
Turn to russet.
Let them bend.

Not your rage.
Not your flesh.
Not your mind.

Feed it with every breath
Fresh.

III: Expire

Like driving your car with the fuel light on
Eventually, it'll jump, then stall.
With no petrol left
Now you have to walk.

X

Coaster

Something to overcome
The taste is there
In the coke and rum.

I swim, and swim, but sink
I drown in it
Can't sip, can't drink.

Too many, you're numb
Drunk. I slip from
Under your thumb.

Stained with rings
Tomorrow you'll
Feel the sting.

Your wildest dreams slipped, I prink
Fool. While you
Take another.

Clink.

X

Iceberg

Your chiselled jawline I admire
Clench your teeth to make it more defined.
Gaze at me with intensity I desire
Steady eyes heavy on me, I resign.

I *almost* regret telling you
How intimidating you were.

Your laugh made your presence shine
The way the skin around your eyes crinkled
The way the sound vibrated down my spine.

You know because I told you
How intimidating you are
So you continued to be
As cold as an iceberg.

You think your power over me is to remain cold
Stubborn to melt, reluctant to move
But my vulnerability with you, lies untold.

An iceberg may have sunk the *Titanic*
But I prefer colliding with something more volcanic.

X

Die Baby, Die

You tell me I look good
As I walk by
But my hair is too short
Try baby, try.

You get closer to me
Hand on my thigh
You tell me you've been patient
Sly baby, sly.

You kiss me gently
Feels like I could fly
Do you think about me often?
Lie baby, lie.

You pulled all my strings
Keys low and high
Did you even mean a thing?
Bye baby, bye.

X

Pea

The only large thing about you was your stature
A man who took pride in his looks
Not at all the kind of heart
Who was interested in a woman and her books.

The only large thing about you was your ego
A man who kept hold of his past
Not at all the kind of heart
Who was interested in something to last.

You kept putting me down
Tried to make me wane.

But you are just a probable pindick
With a pea-sized brain.

X

Lone Wolf

You fight for equality, fists full of mendacity
Lure in your pack, your cavalry.

To me, not a triviality
Weighed heavy, desolately.

False pretences on the night of finality
Future consequences, what a tragedy.

Heart of vivacity, I wait valiantly
I'm red, wrapped in rhapsody, ready for catastrophe.

Casual hearts
Become casualties.

Sit down, child.
Quit crying rampantly, let me feed you reality.

I trust you, ardently … and satirically
I trust you to turn it to travesty.

Charmed by my amity and loyalty
Home of survival and safety
You don't belong here, automatically.
If it's about status, if it's about exclusivity
Your rulebook was my originality
But you cannot mirror personality escapable from captivity.

You trip absently
Beware, your brain began to atrophy
So *that's* how you float in gravity!

Casual hearts
Became casualties.

Sit down, child.
I led the academy of vitality.

X

Your eyes furtive, from your fluctuating fantasy
No lesson left for me to learn, amicably
Full-time through your immaturity
Loved you gallantly, now full of apathy.

The lone wolf howls enthusiastically
Sounder mind over pack mentality.

X

Fanciful

You tell me you're proud
That I've come so far
Yet I ask for your time
Like a wish on a star.

You're over the bridge
Once supported with beams
But the distance too difficult
Fanciful it seems.

You match your shoes to your shirt
But not your words to your deeds
Tell me how we can go on
When you cause collisions with beads?

X

Memory Lane

It's so fascinating to me how you remember the most beautiful things people have done for you. How it made you feel. How you reacted. The excitement in their voice and the grin on their face. Maybe it even makes you think about how many other times someone has treated you that way. Or how special it is, because it's uncommon to share a bond with someone who can make you feel how special you are to them.

If they aren't in your life any more,

Sometimes …

It even makes you miss them.

X

Brick Wall

There are only so many times you can slam your fist against a brick wall before you start to bleed.

Give yourself a break and the blood clots, heals you.
But you keep punching.

The wounds reopen, causing bruising and breaks in your bones. Your fists swell, as if you can feel your heart pulsating. The pain is agonising and gets worse because you keep intensifying your pain. This feeling lasts too long because you're reminded of that whenever you look at your hands. Whenever you feel the sting of running water.

The very same hands that were meant for holding and being held. The same hands that tried to reach out.

But it's not the same as reaching out.

It's not the same when you can look them in the eyes and feel their soul lighten, as you relieve each other of the heaviness that pain brings.

X

Explosive

I woke up to the sound of ticking
Ripped off the blindfold
Suddenly it felt like I had rubbed my eyes too hard
Seeing stars … sparks flying.

Is this really happening?
Sitting on a wooden chair in an empty warehouse
Facing a ticking timebomb.

The walls were white, the ceilings high and my voice echoed.

Who left this in my lap?
How long was I blinded?
Why don't I remember?

The timer, closer to detonation
If this isn't real, I don't want to find out
I couldn't afford to spend more time deliberating.

I turned the explosive around, lifted the back and found three coloured wires:
Red, blue and orange.

Was it ironic the wires were colours of the Armenian flag?
Red, their spilled blood during the genocide
Blue, of the pure sky, and
Orange, representing courage.

Perhaps it was a sign that while I was blinded
My mind needed to be grounded
And my blood was to be spilled if I could not find the courage to survive.

Without another thought, I pulled the orange wire and it snapped.

"*Kaboom,*" I whispered.

X

Last

I never knew the last time I saw you
Would be the last.

Things changed in an instant.

Time passed
Now I wonder when it was that you became a memory.

It is the only thing that lasted.

IV: Express

Strength and vulnerability are closely connected.

X

Do You?

You were sweet, and chivalrous
Do you remember when I did a spin?

You gave me your coat, a bit of your donut
Did you see my widest grin?

You kissed my cheek, looked at me
Did you feel goosebumps on my skin?

You told me someone like me is hard to come by
Do you ever think about what could have been?

You dipped in your toes
Did you notice I jumped all the way in?

X

Strong

Caring about someone and showing them love is what it takes to truly be strong. Why do you keep saying "sorry for crying, sorry for *caring*"? Your compassion is such a gift. Your heart can be bruised like a peach and yet *you still care*. You're strong because you allow them into your heart and trust them not to break it ... And even when they do, you *still* think about how they feel, and how *you* could have done things differently. You're strong because you still love them though feeling hurt. You may be temporarily bruised, but you're a perfectly ripe and sweet peach. With a soft inside, people need to be gentle. But that's what makes you special. It truly is their weakness to not see how rare you are, and yours to not see how your compassion is part of what makes you strong.

X

Two Way Street

She was the fiery red
She had passion, love
She shone bright and then she sped.

I was the white
I was gentle, kind
I saw her coming but was stunned by her light.

It all happened very fast
The red and white splattered
Hitting each other like a crash, creating an enormous blast.

We cried,
Realised our strength is when we collide.

X

Too

If no one has told you yet today,
Allow me to be the first.

You are not too much.

In fact,
You are not *too* anything.

You are not too kind
        too generous
        too …

You'll never be too much for the right people.
You'll never be used or strung along.

Don't be afraid to be yourself.
You don't need validation, you already belong.

Open heart, you love fervently.
Open arms, you give abundantly.

So be yourself,
Because there's no such thing as too soon.

X

I'll Keep

I'll keep ripping out weeds
When they look like flowers.

I'll keep charging against the wind
Until it stops.

I'll keep going through the mess
Until the dark hours.

I'll keep missing you
While your access drops.

There's a promise of better
There's a promise of more.

I'll keep my eyes closed another second
I'll keep trusting God's peace.

Noise turns to silence
Memory release.

X

Stuck

You were going through heartbreak
I couldn't stand idly by and watch
For it was breaking mine too.

I called your mother and organised a time
She helped me decorate your room while you were gone.

I left you and your sister a gift, with a letter
They were interchangeable
I typed them out on my typewriter.

What I wrote came from my heart.
How I cared for you both.

When I went back to your room, I'd still see the Bluetac and remains of the streamers stuck to the corner of your ceiling. I don't remember if I had said anything, but it always made me smile. To know I could make you feel you were special, that you deserved to be loved. That you *were* loved.

Even if it wasn't from someone you wanted to keep in your life.

After a while, when we talked, you told me you'd moved.

I wondered if the new owners:
>Removed the remains of the streamers.
>Thought about why, or what it was there for.
>Gave it a second thought, like I wished you did for me.

X

Another Language

It almost breaks my heart
To look into your eyes
Feeling your love

But it breaks yours
To gaze into mine
Seeing questions

My scent, its taste
Your green light
Intoxicated by your own desire

Hearing noise, seeing red
I stutter at the answers
Reading them like another language.

X

XYZ

It's elementary
Like learning ABC
Smiling at my reflection
Finally feeling *esprit*

Like I'm a sentry
Keeping guard of my own wellbeing
I've done my introspection
Now I'm sight-seeing.

X

Three

Before I leave home I always think about the three things I need.

My phone
My keys
My wallet.

To keep in contact.
To get back home. Where I live. Where I sleep.
To buy food for sustenance. To buy water for thirst.

Some days I may forget one and feel a little itch.
I wonder how people communicated twenty years ago.
I wonder what it's like to not have a home to go back to.
I wonder what it's like to not have money to spend.

I am grateful for the privileges provided to me
By my parents' hard work.

Then I wonder... if I take these objects away.
What are the three things I would need everywhere I go?

The Father
The Son, and
The Holy Spirit.

To keep my relationship.
To protect me. To live. To rest.
To feed my soul. To strengthen me.

X

Gogh

I've fxcked up
I'm not flawless
No returns
I seek solace

You fxcked up
It's too late
Vivid colours
Saturate

Would've told you
Had you wanted to hear
Cut me off like
Vincent Van Gogh's ear

You're not better
She's not worse
Cause of death:
Coerced.

V: Excuse

When you apologise, don't justify the reason.
Otherwise it's like trying to water flowers
With tears during wet season.

X

Dark Night

A dark night
Covered in mystery.
Moonlit, yet
Breathed winds wintry.

I move the clouds
Baring the stars for him.
Suddenly surrounded by crowds, yet
Feel myself dim.

Drawn into the dark
I sink, and slump
Pick myself up, and I feel a spark.

Snapping out, I shone brighter
And lit up the whole sky.
Tell me you've never felt lighter
Just don't tell me I didn't try.

X

Sick

The muscles in your mouth are so well developed
But what about your brain?
You're not what they'd call sick
No bone breaks, no blood stains.

Your illness isn't visible
Just comes straight from your tongue.
If you were like Pinocchio
I could have it wrung.

But people believe what comes from your lips
Because you tell it so well, even you believe it.
Maybe that is what your sickness is
Your sin in saliva, you're a hypocrite.

It took me a while, but now I'm fine
I pinned your insecurity on my blazer like a souvenir.

I hope you get well soon.

Xoxo

Your ex-friend,

Sincere

Water

You can float like a star
You can drown in rough sea
You can get caught in a rip
Or you can water ski.

Dependant on your feeling
Dependant on your responsibility
You either swim or drown in
Understanding your ability.

No safety floats
No paddle, no fins
If water blesses you with new beginnings
If water purifies your sins.

If this was it
If I was going to be immersed
I'm ready for vindication
I'm ready to quench my thirst.

X

Forgive Yourself

Do people even send apology *letters*? How should they start?

> *Dear [your name]*
>
> *I have had time to reflect and deeply comprehend what it was I did wrong. Where I felt I made mistakes.*
>
> *I want to tell you I'm sorry, and I forgive you. You have always been there for me, quite literally. You are too hard on yourself, and your heart is bigger than most. That is why I think it is important for me to acknowledge my error and tell you I am sorry, and I forgive you.*
>
> *You don't deserve to feel pain. You carry many things and dwell too much but I want to remind you, it's okay to make mistakes, as long you learn from them. You can't control the way others react to you, and if they don't stick around, then that's okay too.*
>
> *Forgive yourself. Do you promise?*
>
> *Because I promise to remind you of that, always.*
>
> *Love Janette*

X

Underdog

I've always liked the underdog
Faithful canines.
They bark, can bite
Such a howling delight.

No matter the weather, sunshine or fog
They're a protective blood line.
Too loyal to consider a switch
Rattle them too much, they will snap, twitch.

Yet you still reach out your hand
Canines are cute, so you're distracted.
But you forget you upset them vastly
That their claws cannot be retracted.

I told you they bark
I told you they can bite.
But I didn't tell you their claws can make you bleed
That your scent is what teases their appetite.

Call me the underdog.
Lately I've felt an itch.

Call me the underdog.
Call me a …

X

Stay With Me

Remember when I went to see you in hospital
Thought I'd just drop by.

Hair and makeup done
Dressed to the nines
Ready to have fun.

Walked in to see
You smiled at me.

I didn't know it got this bad
Took one step forward
But feet were stuck.

I turned back
You questioned why I hadn't left
"What do you mean? This is all for you", I professed.

Decided to spend the night
I'm glad I stayed with you
I'm thankful I played with your hair
And said a prayer.

You may have passed away
But I'm glad your love stayed.

The people I had plans with are also gone
Their time for me didn't last much longer
Than the pain that left your body.

Now in solitary
Feeling weary.

The pain entered my body soon after
The only medicine I've got is laughter.

X

Thunder

>When
>You
>Started
>The
>Lightning
>You thought there was no cause and effect.

>>But there's always a
>>Moment of
>>Silence
>>Before
>>The
>>Thunder.

X

Navigate

I'm in troubled waters
Help me find my way.
I've got many anchors
So I drop the weights.

Remind me what they're used for
Remind me I'll be okay.

Waves crashing harder
As I head to the stern.
To find my balance
To finally learn.

Won't go overboard
I am stubborn. I refuse.
Precious cargo to be restored.
Treasure X hidden in the depths
Many layers still unexplored.

X

Prickwork

I had built four walls
Sat smack dab in the centre

You rested beside me
Break and enter

I then stood up
Thrust you out

There are now cracks
I fill with grout.

X

XXXXX

Distance and denial
The perfect combination
An incredulous gasp
Still in adulation.

Red lenses, what a filter
With ruby on the right
And crimson to your left
Red flags are just flags in your sight.

Don't lift your head
Just shift your eyes.

See the diverse dimensions?

Aren't these colours better than all the red lights?

VI: Execute

It will get done, master achiever.
You're not the only one.

X

Little One

You will feel pain, little one
People will hurt you.

Just know
You will always have yourself

Keep your heart pure, and
Look with a gaze straight in front of you

Do not look at those people
Do not engage
Do not let their poison wrap around your wrists
Just so they can tie you down

And if you are stuck, little one
Remedy it by not reacting
Untie yourself and let them go

You are not in control of others
The only thing you need to know is
You are, and always will be
In control of yourself

So keep smiling, little one.

X

Don't

I had spent hours slumped by my bed.
Writing paragraphs, only to cross everything out.

I rested my pen between my lips.
What was I trying to say?

I flicked back a few pages.
The movement of my hand lifted the pen,
Dropping it on the paper.

The ink splotched, right on the sentence that read:
Don't look back.

Spinning

Spinning out of control
Too many thoughts.

Dizzy spin cycle
Stuck to the walls.

Slowing to a halt
Feel like collapsing.

Reaching for a hand
But it keeps slipping.

Opening the door, click
Ready to bolt.

Tripping over my feet
While jumping out.

Holding steady, keen to
Find some stability.

Finally …
Thinking clearly.

Spinning in circles is not for your thoughts, your brain. Spinning in circles is for water, down the drain.

X

Limit

Go beyond the fears and limitations of others
Ignore whoever says you can't.

Ask them why
They'll just tell you again
That you can't.

They think they know the answer
Projecting their self-induced fears
Fear of their own trials
Fear of their own lives.

Or maybe it was something they wished they did
But came to regret they never tried
Either way – it doesn't matter.

Don't let them stop you.

Because you know your heart
And it doesn't stop on a whim
It beats until your final breath.

And when you finally do it …
They'll ask you how.

X

Keep It

Keep it together
But not too much
Gentle with yourself
Like a mother's touch.

You're strong too long
You'll bend
You'll break
Continued crusade
You'll shock
You'll shake.

Friction forms
Ground gets unsteady
Tell yourself next time you wake
You'll be ready.

But can't slow it down
Can't seem to wake up
Keep it together
As it builds up.

Allow the tears
Nothing is wrong.

The strength you have
Has been lifelong.

X

Original

You are as extraordinary as the result of getting photos developed. Perfected in your imperfections overtime. One of a kind.

Until someone wants a duplicate …

Too bad
I've got the original.

X

Protagonist

Just like in every story, there are circumstances the protagonist must overcome. Plot twists, where the protagonist almost gives up but realises their passion is what will make the antagonist back off. That their life is worth fighting for.

Just like in every story, the author chooses who makes it into the next chapter…

Who's in your story?

X

Treasure

X marks the spot.
No matter how long you've searched
Scouring opposite ends of the earth
Digging deep to uncover what you want.

Treasure buried in depths
Otherwise it is not … treasure.
It would be surface level
It would be easily accessible.

If you want to discover treasure

You have got to

        Dig

          Deep.

All you need to do to find your first clue, is face a mirror.

                                      It starts with you.

Puzzle

To solve the puzzle
You need space
Attention to detail
With a slow pace.

Want to see the picture
Want to see what's next
It might feel arduous
You'll be perplexed.

Don't give up
Don't lose motivation
Don't force the puzzle pieces
Or prepare for devastation.

Everyone wants to rush their pain
Everyone wants to find a quick fix
But you can't see the bigger picture
When the puzzle pieces don't mix.

X

Climb

I used to tear myself down to meet you.
But when we would part, I would be itching to climb.

One day I scaled to the top only to see more peaks appear.

If you wish to keep me in your life,

              me.
     with
Climb

VII: Exhale

Let your lungs push the carbon dioxide out.
To make room for you to breathe the oxygen in.

X

Free

Loneliness grips me
Like a shadow seeking a cloud
The calm becomes a storm
Thunder, getting loud.

My mind, trapped beneath the rain
Umbrellas surround me in a crowd
Seek comfort to find my feet are wet
A tightness in my breath, remember I vowed
My feet could bleed yet I still know
It is a measure of my depth – to be proud.

Suddenly lightning
Almost blinding
A spotlight on me.

Its warmth on my face, can barely see
Yet I feel ...

X

Love

Give it time
You'll get used to this
Just like you got used to that
From familiar to new.

Love is not just the one you want to be with
Loss is not just a break up.

Love is giving yourself time to breathe
Love is the way your mother looks at you
Love is the way your father teases you
Love is shown in hugs, and kisses
Love is shown in sibling squabbles.

Look around
Love is everywhere.

You're not in a dark tunnel
You don't have to run that track anymore
You can go off course and watch love in other forms.

True love …
Where love is everlasting
Where love never gives up.

X

Bloom

Don't give me flowers
Don't rip them out from their roots
Just to tell me they're beautiful and
Step on them decomposing with your boots.

Plant a seed in the soil and water it
Watch it slowly reproduce
It'll eventually bloom
Into colours like vermillion and chartreuse.

X

Wild

I don't want you to be wrapped around my finger
I don't want you to be in the centre of my palm
Because rings come off when there's liquor
And I've already got two arms.

No one should exert that much control over you
I want you to be wild and free like the tide
I want you to be yourself, passionate and spritely
Not close my fist and crush you while you're inside.

Bones

My heart beats
Se-cure, fra-gile

It bleeds compassion.

It isn't just worn on my sleeve.

My heart is seen within my eyes
Written on my face
Felt with my hands.

I give you one hundred per cent.
How high does it speak for me to think you do too?

Or for you, is it low?

I learned people do not offer the same capacity you give.

Did you know offering to do something
Is a way to fight in fixing it?

Your heart beats
Un-sure, hurt-ful

It bleeds revenge.

You show me with your actions
You express to me no words
But all you've got
Is a closet full of bones.

X

Archery

I turned away
Decided I had enough.

You drew the string
Aimed at me
Released the bow.

I felt it on my back, it pushed me forward
You used such strength and it pushed me – *forward*.
It may have cut deep and bruised
But it will not stop me from walking away.

Keep aiming at me…
I will show you what it really means to be strong.

I will not turn to look back at you
For I have no interest in seeing behind me.

But you will watch me walk away
For your interest is still on my backside.

X

Music

I've been flicking through music
Perhaps the silence is what I need
Been trying to find the right melody
Been trying not to let it bleed.

He sang a ballad, guitar in hand
Where the words have been stuck in my head
Lyrics fixed on my heart
Its every muscle, its very last shred.

My finger still hovers over the other songs
Regardless of the one that has been here all along
If acoustic was his type, I'm a string
But I'm more into percussion and swing.

X

Inhale

No smoke, pure air
Hold it just a second
With eyes closed
I feel at rest.

Rise and fall with every sigh
Chest expands
With relaxed thoughts
It matters what we ingest.

If seventy per cent of waste
Is eliminated through my lungs
Just by breathing
I'll take deeper breaths.

X

Colours That Don't Exist

Like trying to explain colours that don't exist
How could I let it come to this?

I look up to meet his gaze
His face clouded in a haze.

I break it and as I blink
Can barely see, can barely think.

"I'm sorry," I expel
His hands reach my face
My chin he holds
I whisper, "I need some space."

Purple and blue hues, light up the sky
Make a wish upon a star
This is not goodbye ...

The colour that doesn't exist
I'll call it
Reminisced.

X

Numbers

I do not care for numbers
I do not count the things you do.

If I counted
Perhaps I should have charged revenue.

That's where you're fortunate
If I cared for numbers
I would worry if I were you.

That's where you're fortunate
I do not care for numbers
I do not count the things you do.

Yet you tell me I am one in a billion.

I know. But, okay motherfucker.

I love you too.

VIII: Exude

The better you become, the better you charm.

X

She's The Woman

She's the woman
Who wears strength on her sleeve
No longer naive
She is rid of darkness
Not to be mistaken for heartless
Oh, she wears it well
Eyes soft like a gazelle
Quite the seductress
Tighter than her bodice
She's got you wrapped
Deliberately caught, equally trapped
She is not to be fucked with
Charms shiny like a goldsmith
Oh, she wears it well
Jaw-dropping bombshell.

X

Peach Schnapps

It began like a rose-coloured romance
Time lapse

One act after the other
Made traps

Find where you went wrong
No maps

Now just wait till I walk past you
Neck snaps.

X

Poker

The room filled with smoke, clouding the ceiling.
I inhaled and held my breath.
Just like the films.

I am looking for something, not yet sure what. I exhaled.
The guy on my right flipped his cards as he winked and smirked.
I do not want a Joker.

With my cigarette between my fingers, I lift the glass of whisky.
Where I lifted my glass, the coaster, wet.
I'm not the only one sweating.

As I watch the next player fold, I look across the table.
Dark hair, dark features … peculiarly quiet.
He had been still since the cards were dealt.
I could not seem to stop my gaze.
Even when I looked away, I found myself looking back.

"All in," he pushes in his chips, I hear some crash to the felt.
Everyone threw in their chips and left.
Everyone except him and me.

Once, the room a haze.
Smoke began to dispel from the movement.

He presents a Full House.
Raising my right brow, suddenly the whisky no longer stings.

He fixed my gaze and held it a moment, before flicking a chip in my direction.
I caught it with my right hand, my eyes not moving from his.
"Sh-show me your cards," he stuttered, stunned by my velocity.

"Congratulations," I ignored and raised my glass toward him.
He responded to my gesture by smiling, effectively making me laugh.

X

I looked down at the chip in my hand.

"You have a Royal Flush," he interrupted my thoughts.
This time I was stunned, and he raised his glass.

As senseless as it sounds, I think I found what I was looking for.

Just like the films.

X

Voski
Gold

Though life is outrageous
She remains courageous.

From flat to bumps
To hills she jumps.

Redefining the meaning of giver
She sees a pond and creates a river.

Acting independently, always bold
Silver linings filled with gold.

X

Strawberry Conserve

Slink into the sunlight
Scarlet sleeveless top
Subtly shows my bra
You stare, will not stop.

Silk on my skin
Silhouette of my curves
Glides slow in the wind
Sweet like strawberry conserve.

Stylish in all senses
Slow motion it seems
Inside, full spirited
Outside, sunbeams.

X

Reflection

I read somewhere that you are a reflection of the person to whom you are closest.

If that's true, then I am happy.

For I am:
> Abiding
> Witty
> Alive
> Kind
> Empowering

For the person I am closest to…

Is me.

X

Artist

Beauty in everything you do
From photography to literature.

Putting your dreams on canvas
Painting your future.

An artist tells a story by creation
Their masterpiece is life's duration.

Blue Moon

I don't compete with you
I compete with my past me

Submerging myself to take a breather.

Wanting to better myself
So when asked who I look up to the answer is

Blue moons aren't that common either.

X

Volcano

Is it law that when someone is interested in me based on my appearance, I should automatically be too? But interest with their intent is not something I crave. That sort of interest wanes. After all …

Why would I settle for a ripple in the ocean?

When I prefer the eruptions of a volcano?

X

Magic

Sometimes, like magic, disappearing acts happen.
To face difficult situations
To consider them with a clearer mind
To heal.

Just like magicians,
You surprise your audience when you reappear.

The crowd tries to examine the trick.

No shell of a person
You are confident
Completely recreated.

Your strength isn't an object
Your strength isn't a colour
Your strength isn't an emotion.

Your strength is unbound.

You're resilient.

IX: Explore

Discover your world and define your own meaning
Of being enough, being worthy of love.

Check the clock, to see … it's time.

Overpowering

The most overpowering ache I had ever felt
Was crying out my pain
Was praying to breathe again
Was begging to feel reign.

The most overpowering relief I had ever felt
Was waking from nightmare
Was overcoming gloom
Was breathing in crisp air.

The most overpowering love I had ever felt
Was seeping into my skin
Radiating from every pore
Was a relentless grin
Made me wanting more.

X

Less Is More

Less waiting
More becoming
Hear the melody
Rhythmic drumming.

Unaccompanied feels longer
So immerse yourself
Keep humming.

The more valuable
The more patience
Remain solo.

No instant gratification
Never liked the taste of poison
Toxic release
Tempo increase.

Natural progression
Nothing beats it
Freedom on the verge
Time for the bass to hit.

Beauty

What is the most beautiful thing about someone?
Is it to do with their appearance?

To me, it is their character:
>Their patience with their parents using technology
>Their self-control in the most testing environments
>Their tolerance for someone's small lapse in judgement
>Their loyalty defending friends when they're not around
>Their strong moral principles that never sway.

If you thought of someone as you read this …
Hold onto them.
These qualities are hard to come by.
For they understand beauty isn't just in appearances.
It's in:
>The way you are with others
>The way you make people feel.

Beauty in appearances is a bonus
But it eventually fades.

Beauty is what is in your heart.

X

Spine

They say don't judge a book by its cover.

So I'll tell you
I've felt fire in the hearts of people overlooked
And met others with beautiful faces
Who possess dark souls.

Spine of a book
Like a backbone of the body
Holding everything together
With interleaved pages inside.

When you open it
There's nowhere to hide.

X

Dead Friends

You know something's broken
So you wish to find what.
You look at yourself
And begin to cut.

The tears keep flowing
The blood's pouring out.
But you can't settle
For your pain is not knowing.

You excise to the source
To a heart of glass.
Full of powerful mettle
Full of remorse.

Regret of hurting yourself
Not your kindness to others.

Time to heal
Time to cleanse.

Why do you hurt yourself
Over dead friends?

X

Brain

I can't get my mind to shut off, ticking like the clock on the wall. Thinking all the worst things over again and again …

Why can't I stop thinking about negative experiences?
I lift my phone and look it up.

How could I forget that our brains are wired for survival?

It means that our brain ticks over with negative bias – for purpose. The thought of negative "what ifs" to a situation is simply our mind trying to protect us from something it recognises as traumatic. A reminder to not repeat the experience.

It doesn't mean something is wrong with you. There isn't. It just means it is up to you, how you wish to deal with it.

X

Life

It is there in the word itself: life. Like watching a tree change through seasons. Expanding its roots to grow taller, shed its leaves, only to spring again. Seems like all it takes is the blink of an eye and everything changes.

I vow to make the most of this life.

The older I get the more I realise I could have done more – *lived* more, believed in myself more. If I know this now, why can't I apply that to the present? Even when I look back at what I've accomplished, I *know* I could have done it ... or is that because I already did?

Why does the future hold so much more to fear? Is it because we don't know what it holds, and are afraid of the unknown? Or do we seek to remain where it is comfortable?

I know I will keep reinventing myself, carrying those with me while I ascend. Leaving behind a shadow, in its comfort zone. It might not be easy, but I've learned the hardest things to achieve are the most rewarding and know my life will be just that.

I'm not done yet, I have a long way to go. There are many experiences I am yet to have, people yet to meet.

So here I am.

I vow to believe in my abilities.
I vow to give one hundred per cent.
I vow to *live*.

X

Equation

Solve this problem by finding x.

The duration of pain feels like a long downward spiral, never remembering how long it actually lasts. The same with pleasure. Your mind does not comprehend emotions this way, though we know it was there. We remember the troughs of suffering and the peaks of satisfaction. We remember small setbacks and tiny triumphs, and we always remember how it ends. Just don't elongate its conclusion, because by its end, there's no equity in effort any more. When you know you are facing a heightened emotion, understand that although this feeling is temporary, it is necessary. It is the same as thinking you lost someone, yet you never actually lost anything. You realise you actually gained wonderful moments which turned into memories you won't forget. Don't just exist, explore. Don't just feel it, embrace it. Even when there have been separate incidents affecting you and they feel simultaneous …

Just
Keep
Moving.

How do you do this?

Find the x, read the full sentence where the xs are present.

Add *yourself* to the end.

X

Rain

Why don't you like the rain?

Instead of asking, "Why does it always rain on me?"
Wonder what it will teach you.

Sometimes life is about understanding yourself.
When you feel *x* it means *y*.
When *this* happens, I will react *that* way.

You cannot change or control others
But if *you* don't change, you remain stagnant.

You may never know the reason for people's actions
And they may never apologise because they can't.

Don't hold your breath. Move forward.
You wouldn't wait for a rainy day when you live in the desert.

You'd pursue change.
You'd move.

Seek the rain and pray for it to arrive
To feed your plants and let them grow
So they can survive.

X

Snakes and Ladders

Someone said to me: no matter how many times a snake sheds its skin, it's still a snake
Why didn't I think of that before?
It was as if I'd uncovered a secret code
Like finding a winning strategy.

Then I started deliberating …

Say I was, in a game.
In this case, snakes and ladders.

Sure, the snakes might try drag you down
Hiss at you
But they won't be able to sink their teeth
Take a bite
When your hands are oiled …
Slippery.

In my version of the game, the snakes lose
Or – at least, I don't focus on them
I only see ladders.

X: Exalt

I imagine white lights
No ceilings
No walls

I imagine white clouds
No doors
No falls

Heaven

When I go to heaven
I want to jump in the clouds
Say hello to lost friends
And leave all my doubts.

When I go to heaven
I'll hold my parents' hands
Laugh with my grandfather
While jumping through highlands.

When I go to heaven
I'll inhale the fresh air
Feel nothing but pure bliss
Sometimes I think I'm already there.

X

Dada
Grandfather

You used to push me in my stroller
I said, "Your turn, I'll push you too"
One day
Whenever that day comes to rear my own
I'll smile remembering you.

I close my eyes, wishing you were beside me
Cheering for my triumphs, comforting my defeats
Feel your hand resting on my head
Gently soothing me.

You used to ask me to make you soorj (*coffee*)
I thought I tricked you in saying no
But when I giggled handing you the cup
You handed me a biscuit, and chuckled "dunk"
I dipped it in, quid pro quo.

I close my eyes and feel you're with me
See you dancing to the Charleston
Complete elation, kicking your feet
Sprinkling stardust on me.

"Toon toon toon, im Siranushess"
You you you, my Sweetheart

X

Nana
Grandmother

White petals with yellow centres
You never let me kiss your hands
The hands that raised my mother
The ones that spoke with strong command.

Whenever it's autumn, the leaves fall
Look how beautiful the colours are
We're on our way to see you
Sadly, it was 'au revoir'.
Colour left your cheeks, along with your breath
We wore blue, like the dress you wore to rest
Grief stricken and sick, fine line between life and death
I'm wearing blue by the feeling in my chest.

White petals with yellow centres
My mother hands me a teacup full
Picking the chamomile from my garden
In your blue coat made of wool.
When you pick the chamomile from above
And look down to drop it into your tea
I hope you are watching us
I hope you see.

You never let me kiss your hands
But your blood runs through my mother's veins
So, I hold her hands and kiss them
And hope that it soon rains.

X

Morkouyr Janette
Aunt Janette

The worst pain I had ever felt
Was the feeling of heartbreak.
It was from being in love with, and losing
One whose name I never shared.

What is the worst that could come from pain?
I am now stronger, because I felt, and fought.
I understood what it was like
To feel pain, a loss, I had thought.

It was not until the potential loss of
The one who was there when my mother gave birth to me.
To realise how colossal this is, and
For it to happen days ago, on January three.

The pain constantly reanimating my bones
I've stopped asking why.
For I hope this pain will soon turn to life
As she is now with Jesus, the most High.

Feeling pain, and experiencing loss
Is not weakness, there is no fault or room for blame.
It is in our memories, her legacy
That allows her name to live on, high flame.

The worst pain I have ever felt
Was feeling my heart break.
It was from being in love with, and losing
The one whose name I share.

She is strength, and courage
Who is now looking down.
I am proud to say
I wear our name like a crown.

X

Earth

In my world you are a centrepiece
The scent that makes me smile

In my world you are the bullseye
My focus in a crowd

In my world you are my heart
The warmth that helps me sleep

Earth was once believed to be centre of the universe

But

In my world, you are mine.

X

Baba
Father

My father once said:
When someone knows you will make choices that won't serve their interests, they will lie.
Because they know their truth will provoke you to walk away.

Don't lie, he says
Because you lose character.

Don't just speak, he says
Listen to understand.

Always respect others, he says
And always lend a hand.

When people do wrong to you, he says
Forgive but don't forget.

When it's repeated, he says
Always walk away.

Because you know your morals, he says
Don't end up on a shipwreck, don't be a castaway.

X

Mama
Mother

The sky's a deep sapphire
Your match – you are divine.
Raise your hands and reach
Fresh breath in the alpine.

Let me guide you, close your eyes
Let me make you smile.
I'm never gone too long
I'll make it worthwhile.

Sit beneath the lemon tree
Do you feel my warmth?
Raise your face to mine
A little more north.

It may sometimes storm
I may sometimes be away.
But your rosebuds will be fragrant and grow red
For your beautiful bouquet.

I climb from the coastline
Regardless of the rising moon.
Your flushed skin glistens
Catching my rays trying to croon.

Clouds may deter you
Wind may shiver your spine.
But my warmth for you is day and night
I will always be your sunny sunshine.

X

Minass

I once was in a life raft
The rain was heavy
Waves crashed
The fog was thick
Sea legs like jelly.

I once was in a life raft
The wind swayed
Lights flashing
The lighthouse keeper
The navigational aid.

I once found the shore
Collapsed to the sand
Thunder persistent
Hand on my shoulder
He helped me stand.

I once was in a lighthouse
The keeper, stern
From light reflection
To daymarks and fog signals
Indicators learned.

I once became the keeper
When he had to move away
Keepers quarters
Internal compass strengthened
Better than yesterday.

I once sailed out to sea
I know I'll be fine
Stronger still
Not since been back
Turn to see the light sometimes.

X

Mari

Personality that outshines everything
With a giant brain.
Beauty that draws people in
And humour that entertains.

They adore your magnitude
The way you glisten.
You make everyone feel special
When you speak, they listen.

Your loyalty, supreme
Second biggest, like Saturn.
My childhood hero
Any threats, you'd flatten.

You're a star, a galaxy
Your strength is robust.
Even through the telescope
Making them feel stardust.

X

Home

Home always rich
Bread of life,
Fridge full.

Home always rich
With love all things grow,
Beautiful and pure.

Home always rich
Warm embraces,
Knitted socks of wool.

She whispers with a smile, *your blood is worth bottling*,
It holds more value, the less there is of something.

Home always rich
Irreplaceable,
Priceless.

Home always rich
No matter how far,
My home is in my soul.

X

The variable.
The oxymoron.

Regret

Show them you love them and
Take every opportunity to say it.

There is no such thing as too much, with love.

But there is such a thing as too late.

Silence

Deafening silence
Flood of control
Armoured defence
Out on parole.

Dire suspense
With no patrol
Opposition: dense
With no heart and soul.

The Sistine Chapel

He hands me an envelope with *The Sistine Chapel* in a scribble on the front. I turn the envelope around, open the back and pull out the letter.

Soft white notebook paper with the light blue lines. Ink that you could see from the other side. Like you can see where he hesitated based on how much ink bled through. As I slowly unfold it, I look up at him. He shrugs and his lips move nervously like a twitched smile, but don't open. I keep unfolding the letter until it is straight.

I look down to the letter to hear him softly inhale. The folds created shadows, and there's a rip on the left-hand side. I wonder which notebook he ripped this out of. I wonder how urgent it was to hand me this letter, why it's written about a chapel I haven't been to.

Dear Janette,

I wonder how much thought went into painting the Sistine Chapel because it is so detailed. There are several layers with different brush strokes and diverse colours. It would take a lifetime to appreciate its beauty. Photos and videos of the Chapel could never do it justice… you have to be in its presence. A smart man might tell me there are other paintings to see, but I would rather wait to see it again daily, until I know every detail of its beauty. Because there's nothing I'd appreciate more, and there is nothing more beautiful.

I look up to him as he sighs. He places his hands on mine holding the letter and says, "keep reading".

And so, I keep reading … until the last line:

That's what loving you is like.

She

To know her you must know
She doesn't count favours

Bigger heart than
Any earthquake

Never leaves you behind
She brings you like her Saviour

She's like a radiator
Keep up, keep running
Swoops and overtakes

She's survived too many ends in heart breaks
She's great but she's also not everyone's flavour
Doesn't matter.

Even in heeled boots she'll run acres
To get to you
She'd go from shearers to bakers.

Strangers

We change together
We fall apart

You're a feather
My bleeding heart

We fall together
We change apart

Under the weather
Prediction on chart

Unresolved conflicts
Deep breath, count to ten
Pressure constricts
Friends turn to strangers once again.

Cuddly

A voice, cuddly?
Who would think that someone's voice could be *cuddly*?

The kind of voice that makes you want to
        Reach through the phone
        Embrace them tightly
        Plant a kiss on their soft cheeks.

The kind of voice that
        Calms your mind
        Is your method of meditation
        Sings a lullaby to help you sleep.

The kind of voice that one day
Breaks your heart
When you only hear it through voicemail.

Sometimes

To evade danger
The lady beetle plays dead
The echidna curls into a ball exposing its spines.

I wonder if I'd do something safer.
I wonder what I'd do sometimes.

Sometimes I write
Sometimes I ride
Reaching for the pen under moonlight.

Scratch the surface to be surprised
Fearless in vulnerability
Almost like I'm immunised.

Reflection raising eyebrows
Got my attention
It's just you and me here now.

To evade danger
I wonder if I'd do something safer.
I wonder what I'd do sometimes.

I stare it right in the face
Show it my confines.

Sometimes I write
Sometimes I ride
Tyres screech once I see the green light.

Never one-dimensional
Courage pushing me.

Sometimes I think I'm distilled, like rum.
Sometimes I think I'm an honoree.

Cherry

Interlaced stems leading to crimson
My favourite drupe.

With a scent so sweet
Daring you to have a taste.

Delectable dreams
Fine structure.

Cherry on top's a treat
Don't rush it.
No haste.

Watch her blossom
Transience of life.

Intensity raising the heat
Consistency remains
Leave none of it to waste.

Aveli
More

Magnetic, majestic
Angelically alluring

Memorable, monumental
Authentically assuring

Give you a centimetre
You'll want hectares

Can't wait to meet you
Frequent flares

This story, pending
But there's a hook

You'll want to turn the page
Not close the book.

Pillow

I want to sleep on love and see if it's better than a pillow.

X

Epilogue

I cut out (using control + x) some of my poems from this book. That knot-in-your-gut feeling, wondering whether what you're doing is right. Through my experiences, I've learned not listening to myself has been a detriment, a mistake. As soon as I listened, the knot instantly unravelled. Funny, that.

You might not feel prepared for what's to come, but it doesn't matter. If you wait until you're ready, you will never *be* ready. So be thankful for every painful experience and setback.

I hope wherever you are in your journey, you persevere. Because there is satisfaction in knowing all the delight and dismay you've experienced, was building you for the next stage of your life that will demand a stronger version of you.

It's tough when there are so many relationships, that you feel even the one with yourself is on trial. But life isn't a court case. Treat it like algebra where X represents life, its value... unknown. Only, ignore your mathematics teachers, and seek your own answer. You will never be as young as you are now, so live and revel in your moments, because you never know when it will be the last.

I've learned relationships are like breathing. Inhaling is filling myself with love and exhaling is directing that love toward another. They are both crucial for survival. Think about it. How does it make you feel when you take slow, deep breaths? Calm. Exactly. When you take slow, deep breaths, your brain releases endorphins that have a natural calming effect.

Now imagine if we applied this analogy to our relationships, including the one with ourselves. Imagine the effect it would have if we always tried to be gentle and loving with one another. Although the letter X highlights many variables, the only constant for us is quite simple. It is the comfort in knowing that through change, we always ... exult.

Janette x

A Message For You

The anticipation of action
Consumed by captivation.

Elation creating electricity
Accompanied by authenticity.

Steer from all things faux
Stop waiting for an apology.

To some, there is strength in numbers
To me, preference is integrity.

Focus on finding your miracle
Endeavour and persist.

If mine is lyrical
I hope this assists.

Don't you dare forget
Your existence is clear.

There's plenty you haven't done yet
You matter, and you will *always* belong here.

@janettevoski

www.ingramcontent.com/pod-product-compliance
Lightning Source LLC
Chambersburg PA
CBHW020324010526
44107CB00054B/1965